HEINEMANN STATE STUDIES

Uniquely Wyoming

Larry Bograd

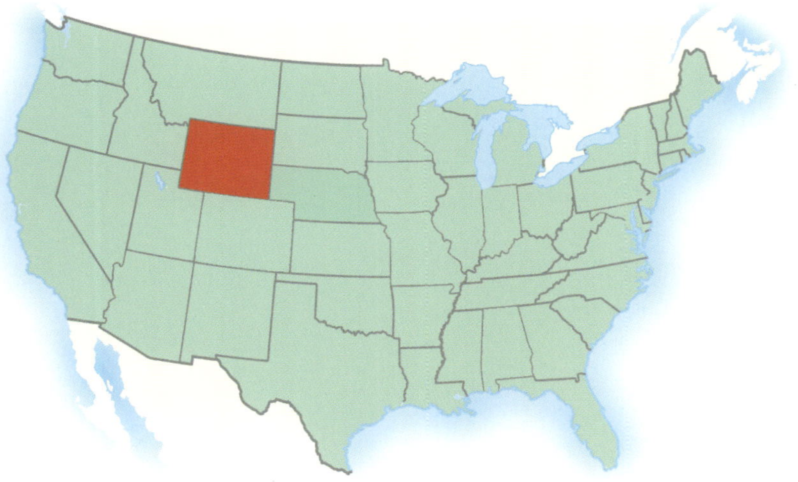

Heinemann Library
Chicago, Illinois

a division of Reed Elsevier Inc.
Chicago, Illinois

Customer Service 888-454-2279

Visit our website at www.heinemannlibrary.com

Designed by Heinemann Library
Printed in China by WKT Company Limited.

08 07 06 05 04
10 9 8 7 6 5 4 3 2 1

Library of Congress Cataloging-in-Publication
Bograd, Larry.
Uniquely Wyoming / Larry Bograd.
p. cm. -- (Heinemann state studies)
Includes index.
ISBN 1-4034-4666-0 (lib. bdg.) -- ISBN 1-4034-4735-7 (pbk.)
1. Wyoming--Juvenile literature. I. Title. II. Series.
F761.3.B64 2004
978.7--dc22

2004002777

Cover Pictures

Top (left to right) Cheyenne's Frontier Days, wolf, Wyoming state flag, snowboarder
Main pond at Mammoth Hot Springs in Yellowstone National Park

Acknowledgments
Development and photo research by
BOOK BUILDERS LLC

The author and publishers are grateful to the following for permission to reproduce copyrighted material:

Cover photographs by (top, L–R): Photo by Jim Pickerell/Alamy; Louise Murray/Alamy; Joe Sohm/Alamy; James Kay/Alamy (main): Andre Jenny/Alamy.

Title page (all): Photos by Wyoming Travel & Tourism; p. 5 Courtesy Casper Area Convention & Visitors Bureau; p. 6, 10, 16, 19 American Heritage Center, University of Wyoming; p. 7 Stephen Saks/Index Stock Images; p. 8T, 9, 11, 14T, 14M, 15B, 38, 39, 42, 43, 44 Courtesy Wyoming Travel & Tourism; p. 8B, 40, 45 IMA for BOOK BUILDERS LLC; p. 12T Joe Sohm/Alamy; p. 12B One Mile Up; p. 13, 15T Gary M. Stolz/USFWS; p. 14B Lloyde Hazzard/USFWS; p. 17T Culver; p. 17B, 36 Courtesy BLM Wyoming/Trails Center; p. 18, 20B AP Wide World Photos; p. 20T AP Photo/Jerry T. Mosey; p. 21 Courtesy The White House; p. 22 Andre Jenny/Alamy; p. 23T Graeme C. Colmer; p. 23B Louise Murray/Alamy; p. 25T, 25B Courtesy Cheyenne Area Convention & Visitors Bureau; p. 28 Eliot Cohen; p. 27 Jim Pickerell/Alamy; p. 29 Courtesy of the Cattlemen's Beef Board & National Cattlemen's Beef Association; p. 30 Ansen Seale for thunderheartbison.com; p. 32 John Stehn/USFWS; p. 33, 34 Courtesy UW Sports Information Office; p. 35 James Kay/Alamy.

Special thanks to Laura Lee Lake, a Wyoming educator, for her expert comments in the preparation of this book.

Every effort has been made to contact copyright holders of any material reproduced in this book. Any omissions will be rectified in subsequent printings if notice is given to the publisher.

Some words are shown in bold, **like this.** You can find out what they mean by looking in the glossary.

Contents

Uniquely Wyoming 4

Wyoming's Geography and Climate 6

Famous Firsts 9

Wyoming's State Symbols. 12

Wyoming's History and People 16

Yellowstone National Park 22

Wyoming's State Government 24

Wyoming's Culture 27

Wyoming's Food 29

Wyoming's Folklore and Legends. 31

Wyoming's Sports Teams 33

Wyoming's Businesses and Products 36

Attractions and Landmarks 39

Map of Wyoming 45

Glossary 46

More Books to Read. 47

Index. 48

About the Authors 48

Uniquely Wyoming

Unique means one of a kind. Wyoming, the ninth-largest state in area, is unique in many ways. It has the nation's smallest population, with less than 500,000 people. Long before it became a state in 1890, the Wyoming Territory gave women the right to vote in 1869—51 years before the entire United States did so. Located in the western United States, Wyoming is bordered by Montana, South Dakota, Nebraska, Colorado, Utah, and Idaho. Wyoming has the second-highest **elevation** in the nation—only Colorado has a higher average elevation.

Origin of the State's Name

The name *Wyoming* comes from the Delaware Native American word *mscheweamiing* meaning "large plains." Plains are flatlands. Wyoming is mostly plains with ranges of towering mountains.

Major Cities

Cheyenne is Wyoming's state capital and largest city, with 53,000 residents. Cheyenne was founded in 1867, when the Union Pacific Railroad passed through on its way to the West Coast. General Grenville Dodge, who led the railroad construction, named the new town after the Cheyenne Native Americans in the area.

Laramie is Wyoming's third-largest city, with about 27,000 people. It was named for Jacques La Ramie, a French-Canadian fur trapper. La Ramie set off for the mountains in the fall of 1820 and was never seen again.

Laramie, located 50 miles northwest of Cheyenne, is home to the University of Wyoming. White Hall, a **dormitory,** is the tallest building in the state at just twelve stories high. Laramie is also home to the world's largest bronze bust—a sculptured head of Abraham Lincoln. It is twelve feet high and weighs three tons—about as much as a large car. Robert Russin, an art professor at the University of Wyoming, made the bust in 1959. The statue marks the highest point on the Lincoln Highway, which was the first **transcontinental** highway.

Located near the center of the state, Casper is Wyoming's second-largest city. It is home to about 52,000 people. It was named after nearby Fort Caspar, but the clerk who filed the town's plans in 1888 misspelled the name.

The city of Casper was named in honor of U.S. Army officer Caspar Collins. He was killed in 1865 during a battle with Native Americans at Platte Bridge Station.

Wyoming's Geography and Climate

Wyoming's land and climate vary greatly. There are snowy, mountainous regions in the middle of the state and large areas of flatlands where the temperature can rise up to more than 100°F in the summer.

Until the late 1880s, bison could be found all across the Great Plains. Hunters were hired by the railroad to shoot and kill thousands of the animals. Today, the bison population is increasing due to the efforts of the state's conservationists.

Land

Wyoming is divided into three major land regions—the Great Plains, the Rocky Mountains, and the Intermontane Basin.

The eastern half of Wyoming is part of the Great Plains. Ranches dot this vast, flat land. The native grasses of the area provide food for cattle and other livestock.

The Rocky Mountains cut across Wyoming from the northwest to the south-central border. Their peaks form the **continental divide** of North America.

The third major land region in Wyoming is the Intermontane Basin. *Intermontane* means "between the mountains." These areas, or basins, receive less rain and snow than the mountains, and few trees grow in the region. Wyoming's principal basins are the Bighorn and Powder River Basins in the north, the Wind River Basin in central Wyoming, and the Washakie, Green River, and Great Divide Basins in the south.

Climate

At 6,700 feet above sea level and far from any ocean, the air in Wyoming is dry, or semiarid. Wyoming's high **elevation** tends to create a relatively cool climate, or average condition of weather over a period of time, in the state, especially at night. Because of the elevation and low humidity, the land does not retain much of the heat from the sun. On the Great Plains, however, summer temperatures can easily exceed 100 °F.

Because Wyoming's land regions vary from high mountains to basins, the amount of precipitation—rain or snow—differs from place to place. Overall, Wyoming averages only thirteen inches of rain or snow each year. Desert areas receive as little as 5 inches of rain each year, while the mountains may receive more than 200 inches of snow each year.

The Continental Divide

Every continent has a continental divide—a line of high mountain peaks that mark the place where the continent's rivers flow in opposite directions. In Wyoming, the Platte, Big Horn, and Yellowstone rivers east of the divide drain east into the Missouri River Basin, eventually joining the Atlantic Ocean. The Snake River, on the west side of the divide, drains west into the Columbia River, eventually joining the Pacific Ocean. Hikers in Wyoming's mountains can stand with one foot on either side of the "Great Divide."

The Red Desert

Located in a remote basin area of southwestern Wyoming, the Red Desert contains dried, red-bottomed lakes dotted with a spiny shrub called greasewood, towering **buttes,** shifting sand dunes, and fossil beds from an ancient inland sea. It is home to the largest pronghorn antelope herd in the lower 48 states.

Average Annual Precipitation Wyoming

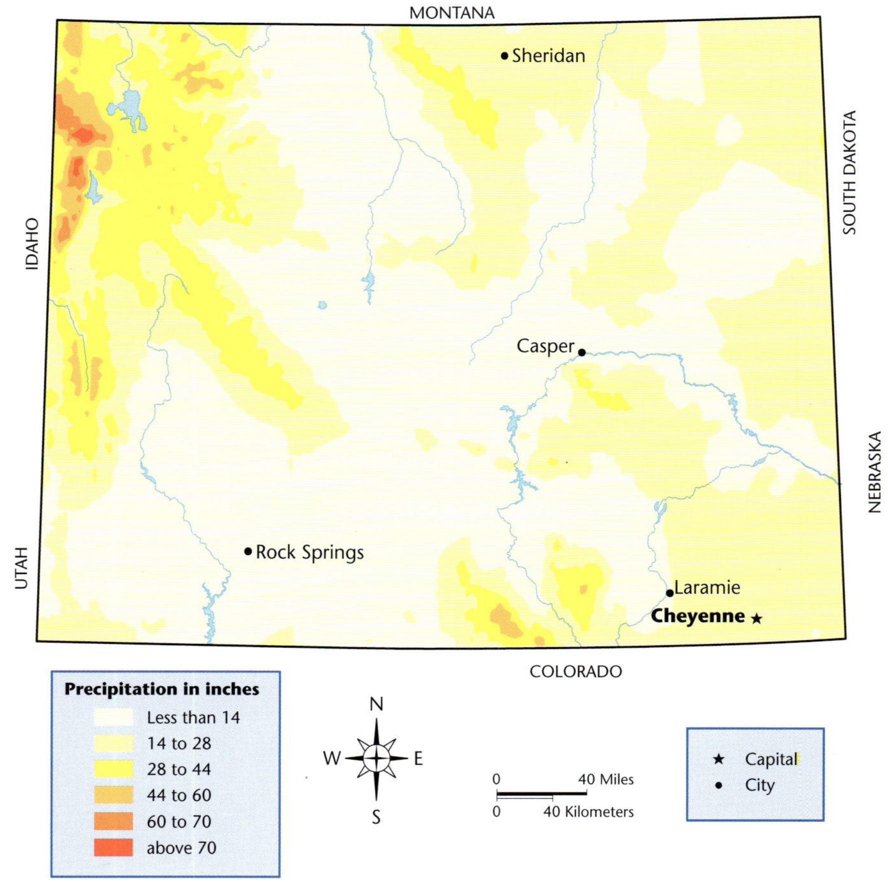

While the basins of central Wyoming receive little precipitation, the Rocky Mountains in the northwest can get more than 100 inches.

Famous Firsts

The West

In 1834 William Sublette and Robert Campbell built Fort William, one of the first large trading posts west of the Missouri River. The exact location of Fort William is unknown, but it was built near where the Laramie and North Platte rivers meet. At the post, pioneers and Native Americans bought and sold goods. Several **treaties** were signed there as well.

An 1872 act of Congress made Yellowstone the first national park in the United States. Signed into law by President Ulysses S. Grant, the act marked the nation's commitment to preserving parts of the wilderness for generations to come.

The first dude ranch in Wyoming was the Eaton Ranch, near Wolf, which opened in 1879. The Eatons also came up with the term *dude,* meaning an Easterner or city person who vacations in the West. A dude ranch introduces city people to ranch life and gives them a chance to wear western clothes and ride horses. Dude ranches make western states a popular destination for people from other states and countries.

Yellowstone Park spreads over the corners of three states. Ninety percent of the park is in Wyoming and the rest is in Montana and Idaho.

In 1891 President Benjamin Harrison selected Shoshone National Forest as the country's first national forest. Later that year, the first ranger station was established in the Shoshone Forest. A national forest is protected against excess logging, allowing most of the trees to grow and die according to natural cycles. Wyoming now has nine national forests.

Devils Tower was designated as the first national monument in 1906 by President Theodore Roosevelt. It was once hidden below the earth's surface, but centuries of **erosion** stripped away the softer rock layers, leaving a steep rock tower rising 1,267 feet above the ground. The area is a sacred site for many Native Americans.

In 1902 James Cash Penney opened his first store in the town of Kemmerer. He named it the "Golden Rule" because he wanted his customers to know that they would be treated fairly. In time the single store grew into a national chain owned by the J.C. Penney Company. By 1928 Penney's owned 1,023 stores and enjoyed yearly sales of more than $175 million. Penney's business became the model for today's large retail chains such as Wal-Mart and Kmart.

J.C. Penney kept his first store open from sunrise to sundown to attract as many customers as possible.

Firsts for Women

In 1869 Wyoming became the first place to grant women the right to vote in territorial elections. The following year, Esther Hobart Morris was appointed the first

Buffalo Bill Dam and Historical Center

In 1905 the U.S. government decided to build the highest dam in the world near Cody, Wyoming, to help farmers and ranchers store water to use during dry periods. The Buffalo Bill Dam was named after the western showman William "Buffalo Bill" Cody, who founded the town of Cody in 1896. When completed in 1910, the dam stood 325 feet tall. Buffalo Bill Dam was added to the National Register of Historic Places in 1973. The Buffalo Bill Historical Center, minutes away from the dam, is one of the most important museums on the American West.

female justice of the peace in the United States. That same year the first all-woman jury was seated in Laramie, and Mary Atkinson was appointed the first woman **bailiff** in the world.

In 1920 the northwestern Wyoming city of Jackson became the first town in the United States to be led entirely by women. From 1920 to 1921 it had a female mayor, town council, and town marshal. To achieve this first, one of the councilwomen defeated her husband for her council seat.

Other Famous Firsts

Wyoming was the first state to have a county public library system, when Laramie County opened its own in 1886.

The first high school football game to be played at night using electric lights took place in Midwest, Wyoming, in 1925.

Wyoming's State Symbols

Verna Keyes of Casper designed the Wyoming state flag in 1917.

Wyoming State Flag

The red border of the Wyoming flag represents the Native American people and the blood of the pioneers. White represents snow and purity. Blue is the color of the sky and mountains. In the center of the flag is a silhouette of a bison, the state mammal. The state seal is centered on the bison silhouette.

The one-sided state seal, adopted in 1893, appears on official state documents.

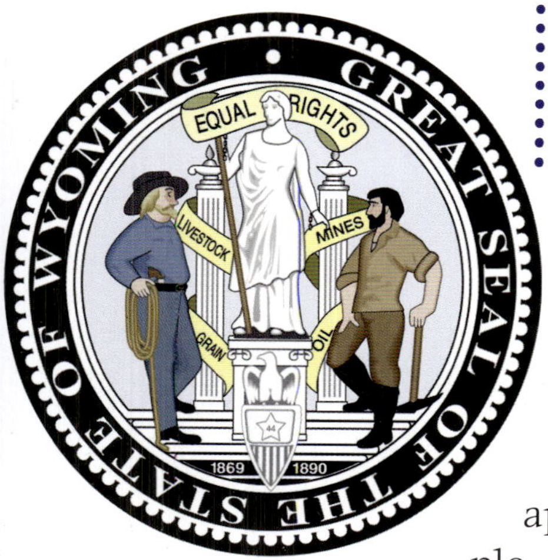

Wyoming State Seal

The two dates on the Great Seal of Wyoming, 1869 and 1890, refer to the year its territorial government went into effect and the year it became a state, respectively. The 44 on the 5-pointed star means that Wyoming was the 44th state admitted to the Union. The scrolls that wrap around the two pillars bear the words *oil, mines, livestock,* and *grain*—four of Wyoming's major industries.

State Motto: "Equal Rights"

"Equal Rights" is the state motto, and it appears on the state seal. It reminds people of the political freedom that women have long enjoyed in Wyoming.

State Nicknames

Wyoming has three official nicknames. "Equality State" speaks to its pride in being a leader in establishing a woman's right to vote. "Big Wyoming" and "Cowboy State" refer to its vast, open spaces and its many ranches and western traditions.

State Song: "Wyoming"

During the summer of 1903, Judge Charles E. Winter of Encampment wrote a poem titled "Wyoming." George Edwin Knapp, a music professor at the University of Wyoming, composed a melody for the poem. His version was first played at a Wyoming State Teachers' meeting, and it became the state song in 1955.

"Wyoming"

In the far and mighty West,
Where the crimson sun seeks rest,
There's a growing splendid State that lies above,
On the breast of this great land;
Where the massive Rockies stand,
There's Wyoming young and strong, the State I love!

Chorus

Wyoming, Wyoming! Land of the sunlight clear!
Wyoming, Wyoming! Land that we hold so dear!
Wyoming, Wyoming! Precious art thou and thine!
Wyoming, Wyoming! Beloved State of mine!

State Flower: Indian Paintbrush

The Indian paintbrush received its colorful name because it resembles an artist's brush touched with yellow or red paint. It became the state flower in 1917. The Chippewa used the Indian paintbrush as a medicine and as a rinse to make their hair shiny.

The Indian paintbrush is a wildflower that grows throughout Wyoming.

The wood of the cottonwood was an important building material in the pioneer days. Settlers used it to build barns and houses.

State Tree: Cottonwood

Common in Wyoming, the cottonwood became the state tree in 1947. Its bark is gray and its leaves are long and triangular with slightly jagged edges. Cottonwoods often grow along rivers and creeks. The trees' root systems find water in dry places. They grow quickly and usually live between 70 and 120 years.

The western meadowlark is a songbird about the size of a robin.

State Bird: Western Meadowlark

The western meadowlark became the state bird in 1927. It lives in the open, makes its nests on the ground out of dried grasses, and eats mostly insects and spiders. Both parents care for newly hatched offspring for the eleven or twelve days that the young stay in the nest.

State Fish: Cutthroat Trout

The cutthroat trout became the state fish in 1987. Belonging to the same family as salmon, the cutthroat trout is spotted and has two red slashes on its lower jaw, which explains its name.

The cutthroat trout can grow to 30 inches long and weigh more than 40 pounds. It is the only trout native to Wyoming.

State Reptile: Horned Lizard

Adopted as the state reptile in 1993, the flat-bodied horned lizard eats ants. It blends in so easily with its surroundings that it is hard to see, which helps it from being eaten by larger animals.

The horned lizard is sometimes called a horned toad, but it is not a toad.

State Mammal: Bison

The bison became the state mammal in 1985. Bison weigh between 800 and 2,000 pounds and stand nearly 6 feet high at the shoulder. Bison feed on grasses. Bison can reach speeds of up to 30 miles per hour, about as fast as a car on a city street. Bison live about fifteen years.

Today only 200,000 bison remain in the United States, with just 16,000 roaming in the wild. Yellowstone National Park has the only population of truly free-roaming bison.

State Dinosaur: Triceratops

Triceratops lived about 65 to 70 million years ago in what is today Montana, North Dakota, South Dakota, Wyoming, and the Canadian provinces of Saskatchewan and Alberta. This enormous, plant-eating beast weighed up to twelve tons—as heavy as a large truck. It became the state dinosaur in 1994.

State Gemstone: Jade

Wyoming jade is black, green, gray, or white. Green jade was discovered in 1936 near the town of Lander. People rushed to central Wyoming to find green jade because it was a valuable gem. In the summer of 1945, collectors removed more than 7,000 pounds of jade.

Wyoming's History and People

Wyoming's history goes back thousands of years, long before the first European explorers arrived. Scientists in Wyoming have found **artifacts,** such as arrowheads and pieces of pottery, which may be 12,000 years old. Little is known about the ancient people who created these artifacts.

After years of conflicts between settlers and Native Americans, the Plains peoples were forced to move to reservations—land set aside by the national government. Wind River, the only reservation in Wyoming, is home to about 6,000 Shoshone and Arapaho.

Native Peoples

Among the Native Americans who lived in what is today Wyoming were the Arapaho, Blackfoot, Cheyenne, and Crow. In the 1800s the Sioux, Shoshone, and Ute moved to the area and replaced most of the earlier tribes. Often called the Plains peoples, these tribes remained in Wyoming until they were defeated by new settlers and the U.S. Army.

Early Explorers

In 1807 John Colter became the first European explorer in the area. A member of the Lewis and Clark expedition sent by President Thomas Jefferson in 1804 to explore

During the 1800s thousands of settlers traveled the Oregon Trail to live in the western states, such as Wyoming.

newly acquired western lands, Colter set off on his own. He explored northwest Wyoming, the area that would later become Yellowstone National Park. In the early 1820s and 1830s, **mountain men** and trappers came to the area, catching beavers and other animals. They sent the **pelts** back to eastern states where they were made into fashionable men's hats.

The ruts of the Oregon Trail were designated a National Historic Landmark in 1966.

After **prospectors** discovered gold in California in 1848, people from all over the world headed there, hoping to strike it rich. Soon, wagon trains carrying gold seekers rolled through Wyoming on the **Oregon Trail** or the **California Trail.** So many wagons used the trails that they left ruts two to six feet deep in the soft sandstone of southeastern Wyoming.

Slowly, the fur trade declined. Many former trappers settled along the trails, providing horses and supplies to newcomers. Native Americans, who feared that the white settlers would take away their lands, battled the U.S. Army. Although **treaties** tried to end the killing, many bloody battles were fought in what is today Wyoming. U.S. troops drove the remaining Sioux north into Montana or Canada or moved them to reservations. Eventually, cattlemen began setting up huge ranches on the land that formerly belonged to Native Americans.

The Mormon Trail

The **Mormons,** a religious group that moved west seeking freedom from persecution, used a wagon trail that led to Salt Lake City, in present-day Utah. This trail became known as the Mormon Trail. In 1856 two Mormon parties were trapped in a blizzard in what is now Wyoming. About 200 people died of hunger and cold before rescuers from Salt Lake City found the survivors.

The Railroads

By 1870 about 350,000 people had traveled westward across Wyoming. By that time, the wagon train had been replaced by the new coast-to-coast Union Pacific railroad, which was completed in 1868. In the 1870s the building of the railroads led to the creation of new towns such as Cheyenne, Laramie, and Rock Springs. Railroad companies laid track and put up buildings. They also owned huge tracts of land that they had received from the government. The railroads offered to sell these lands to pioneers. To encourage settlement, they published brochures about the lands for sale. These brochures provided descriptions of the West and included information about crops and livestock.

Throughout the 1860s, large construction crews laid the tracks for the Union Pacific railroad.

Statehood

Wyoming became the 44th state in 1890. It was also the first state in the Union to allow women the right to vote. Wyoming was also one of the first states to adopt the **secret ballot**.

At birth, Washakie, the future chief of the Shoshones, was named Pina Quanah, which means "smell of sugar."

Famous People

Washakie (c. early 1800s–1900), Shoshone chief. Washakie's name means "shoots on the run." After leading his tribe through several battles, Washakie decided that fighting the settlers would not help his people. He began to help the U.S. Army against other tribes, especially the Sioux and Cheyenne. In exchange, the government built schools and churches for the Shoshone. He was buried with full military honors at Fort Washakie.

June Etta Downey (1875–1932), psychologist. Born in Laramie, June Etta Downey graduated from the University of Wyoming in 1895. She went to the University of Chicago, where she received a master's degree in philosophy and psychology. She returned to the University of Wyoming and became a professor. She was one of the first psychologists to treat the study of human personality as a science.

Nellie Tayloe Ross (1876–1977), governor. Nellie Tayloe Ross, born in St. Joseph, Missouri, moved to Cheyenne in 1902. Her husband, William B. Ross, was elected as Wyoming's governor in 1922. After he died in office in 1924, the Democratic Party nominated Mrs. Ross to complete her husband's term. She easily won the election and thus became the first woman governor in the United States, serving until 1927. Later, President Franklin D. Roosevelt chose Ross as director of the U.S. Mint, a position she held until 1953. She died in 1977 at the age of 101.

Jackson Pollock (1912–1956), painter. Born in Cody and determined to become a world-famous painter, Jackson Pollock moved to New York in 1929 and studied painting at the Art Students' League. Over time, he developed his own style. By the mid-1940s he no longer used a brush but dripped and splashed paint onto a canvas stretched on the floor. This approach was called "action painting" and resulted in busy **abstract** designs that took up the entire canvas. During the mid-1950s he was one of the most famous artists in the United States.

Jackson Pollock's style was a big change from painters who painted people or landscapes.

Curt Gowdy (1919–), broadcaster. Born in Green River, Curt Gowdy's first job as a radio sportscaster was in 1944. He stood on an orange crate in Cheyenne and described a six-man football game played before a crowd of fifteen people in subzero weather. For many years, he called games for the Boston Red Sox. In his career he called thirteen World Series, sixteen All-Star games, the Super Bowl, and the Olympics for fans watching on television.

When asked about being a sportscaster, Curt Gowdy (left) said, "I tried to pretend that I was sitting in the stands with a buddy watching the game—poking him in the ribs when something exciting happened."

Alan Simpson (1931–), senator. Born in Denver, Colorado, Alan Simpson moved to Cody as a boy. He was a local and state official before being elected to Congress. Simpson served as one of Wyoming's U.S. senators from 1979 to 1997. From 1985 to 1995 his fellow Republican senators elected him as their whip, the second-highest position within the party in the Senate. As whip, Simpson was responsible for promoting Republican causes in Congress and to the public.

Dick Cheney (1941–), politician. In the late 1960s Dick Cheney moved from Wyoming to Washington, D.C., and worked for President Richard M. Nixon. In 1975, at age 34, he became the White House chief of staff to President Gerald R. Ford. After Ford left office, Cheney was elected to the U.S. House of Representatives, where he served six terms. In 1989 President George H. W. Bush selected Cheney as secretary of defense. When Texas governor George W. Bush ran for president in 2000, he selected Cheney to be his vice president.

Born in 1941, in Lincoln, Nebraska, Dick Cheney grew up in Casper and later attended the University of Wyoming.

Yellowstone National Park

Yellowstone is the oldest national park in the country and is perhaps Wyoming's most famous landmark.

Millions of people enjoy the natural beauty of the park at places such as this pond near Mammoth Hot Springs.

Yellowstone's History

In the 1860s photographs of Yellowstone appeared in eastern newspapers. People realized the uniqueness of the area. In 1872 Congress passed a **bill** that made Yellowstone the world's first national park. The bill, signed by President Ulysses S. Grant, sought to preserve Yellowstone as a "pleasuring-ground for the benefit and enjoyment of the people."

The Park

Yellowstone contains forests, rivers, cliffs, meadows, and more than 300 **geysers.** The park sits on one of the country's "hot spots," where **magma** seeps from the earth's core toward the surface. The high heat from the rock causes underground water to boil and shoot up from the surface. Elsewhere in Yellowstone, minerals have turned pools of bubbling mud into colorful "paint pots."

Old Faithful erupts about every hour and a half for up to five minutes, shooting a column of steam and hot water as high as a five-story building. About 10,000 to 12,000 gallons of water shoot up every time Old Faithful erupts. That is the same amount of water that is used by flushing a toilet more than 7,000 times.

THE PARK TODAY

More than four million people visit Yellowstone Park each year. The park is huge—more than 2.5 million acres—and spills into neighboring Idaho and Montana. The Grand Loop, Yellowstone's major road, stretches for more than 140 miles in an immense figure eight. The park includes more than a thousand miles of trails for hiking and horseback riding, and it has lakes and streams for fishing or boating. Yet there are places in Yellowstone without a single human footprint.

Reintroducing the Wolf

Wolves were once native to the Yellowstone area. In the 1900s, however, ranchers living near Yellowstone killed wolves that attacked their cattle, sheep, and other farm animals. By the 1930s wolves were gone from Yellowstone National Park. In 1995 officials decided to reintroduce the wolf to the park. They wanted to restore the natural balance in Yellowstone, allowing the wolf to once again control the population of certain plant-eating animals. Thirty-one gray wolves were brought to Yellowstone from Canada and set free.

Wyoming's State Government

Wyoming's state government is modeled after the U.S. government. It has three branches: the legislative branch, the executive branch, and the judicial branch.

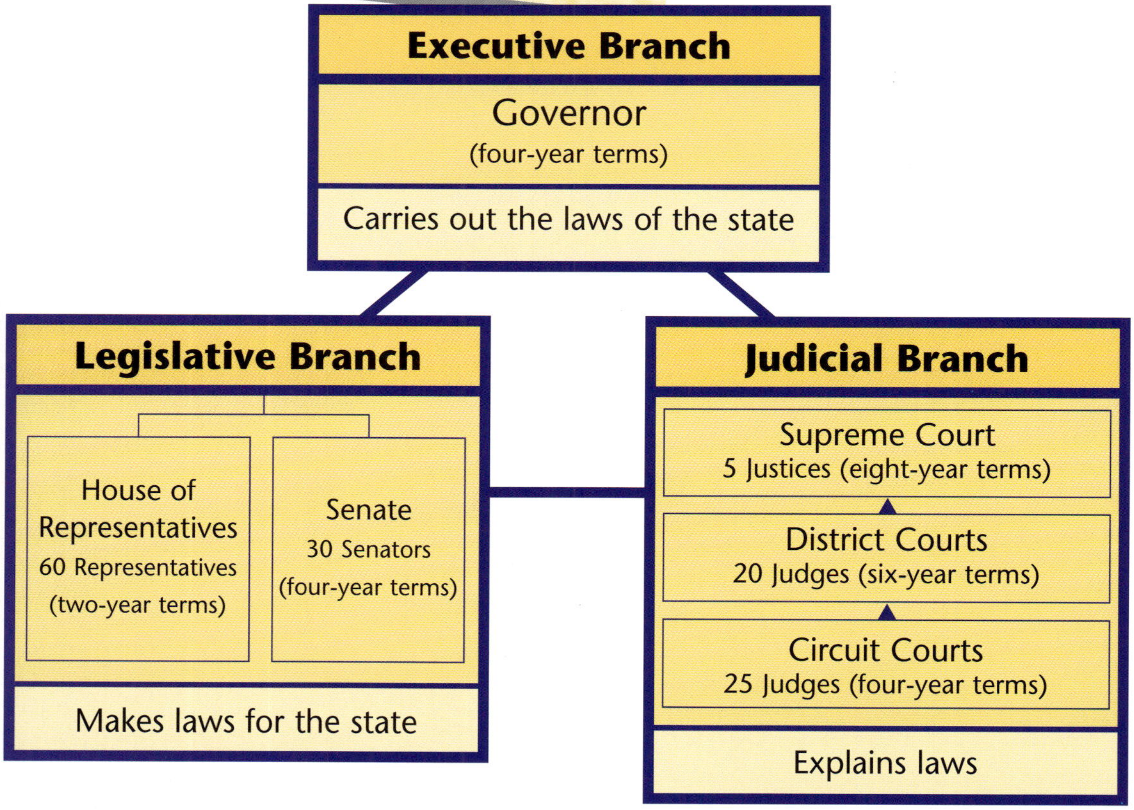

Legislative Branch

Wyoming's **legislature** makes the laws for the state. The legislature is divided into two houses. The larger body, called the house of representatives, has 60 members. Representatives are elected to two-year terms and may serve a total of twelve years. The smaller body, which has 30 members, is known as the senate. State senators are elected to four-year terms and may also serve no more than twelve years.

Legislators propose **bills** during their sessions. For a bill to become a law, a **majority** of the legislature must approve it. The governor either signs the bill into law or **vetoes** it. If he or she vetoes the bill, the legislature may **override** the veto if a two-thirds majority of each house approves it.

A statue of Esther Hobart Morris stands outside Wyoming's capitol building. Morris was a leader in the movement to give women the right to vote.

Executive Branch

The executive branch is led by the governor, who is elected to a term of four years. The governor may not serve more than two four-year terms in any four-term period. Voters also elect the secretary of state, the auditor, and the treasurer to help the governor run the state. The governor, however, appoints the attorney general and other people to head the state's executive departments.

Judicial Branch

The judicial branch interprets Wyoming's laws. Wyoming has three levels of state courts: the circuit courts, the district courts, and the Supreme Court.

Twenty-five circuit courts serve the state. These courts hear cases that do not involve more than $7,000. Circuit courts also hear family violence cases and misdemeanors, or lesser crimes. The governor appoints circuit court judges to four-year terms.

Cheyenne is the capital of Wyoming. It is located in the southeastern corner of the state, only 10 miles from Colorado and 40 miles from Nebraska.

The district courts are the trial courts of the state. District judges hear **criminal cases** and **civil cases** as well as **appeals cases** from the lower courts. The twenty district judges hear cases in nine judicial districts. District judges are chosen by the governor from a list of three qualified persons submitted by the Judicial Nominating Commission. After serving on the court for one year, the new judge runs for election on a statewide ballot at the next general election. If a majority votes in favor of the judge, he or she serves the remainder of the term. The judge may run for succeeding terms on a **nonpartisan** ballot. Judges serve six-year terms and must retire by age 70.

The Wyoming Supreme Court, located in Cheyenne, is the highest court in the state. Its decisions are final, except for certain cases that can be appealed to the U.S. Supreme Court. Most cases that come before the Wyoming Supreme Court are appeals from the lower courts. The Supreme Court also regulates the practice of law in the state. The five justices of the Supreme Court serve eight-year terms. They are chosen in the same manner as district court judges. Justices must retire by age 70. The five justices select the chief justice, who serves a four-year term.

Wyoming's Culture

Culture is an area's blend of history, geography, food, music, art, and the people who live there. Ranch life is central to Wyoming's culture, as is true for other western states. In honor of its ranch culture, Wyoming hosts the world's largest rodeo.

Cheyenne Frontier Days

Frontier Days, the country's largest rodeo, takes place for ten days every July in Cheyenne. It is nicknamed the "Daddy of 'em All" because of its size and importance on the professional rodeo circuit. The first Frontier Days rodeo in 1897 attracted 15,000 people. Today more than 300,000 visitors from all 50 states and many foreign nations enjoy the festivities. During Frontier Days the state population temporarily increases by 60 percent.

Hundreds of boomtowns simply closed up when the gold or silver was gone and jobs disappeared.

Wyoming's Ghost Towns

Hundreds of prospectors flocked to Wyoming after the news of a gold or silver strike. In search of riches, these folks claimed a plot of land and lived in tents. Other people followed the prospectors to sell food, clothing, or equipment. Small towns sprang up almost overnight. These places became known as boomtowns because they "boomed" during the gold and silver rush. Today these ghost towns dot the west. Wyoming's most famous ghost town is South Pass City. When gold was discovered near South Pass City in 1867, more than 2,000 people moved there within a few months. Located in the Wind River Mountains, South Pass City was once a bustling town with about 300 buildings. Today it is a state historic site. South Pass City's remaining 39 buildings give a glimpse into Wyoming's boom-and-bust era.

Wyoming's Food

Food unique to Wyoming comes from its ranching tradition. Beef is the food that is most characteristic of the state. Ranchers and cowboys have eaten beef since the frontier days of the Old West.

Chuck Wagon Cooking

A chuck wagon, a kitchen on wheels, rode ahead of the cowhands as they drove a herd of cattle north. The chuck wagon served hearty meals—beans, bacon, beef, black coffee, and dried apples or prunes—to hungry cowhands. Chuck wagon meals were not fine cooking, but they were hot and filling. The cook dished out the meal, and the cowhands ate around a campfire under the stars. Charles Goodnight, a Texas rancher, is credited with inventing the chuck wagon in 1866.

Beef

Wyomingites' favorite food is beef. People use beef for hamburgers, barbecues, pot roasts, or steaks. The state

Steak was a Wyoming favorite during the 1800s and continues to be popular today.

has hundreds of cattle ranches. Recently some ranches have added bison to their herds. Bison meat has more protein and less fat than beef.

Buffalo Chili

Here is a Wyoming recipe that feeds a dozen hungry people. **Be sure to have an adult help you.**

3 pounds ground bison meat
1 chopped onion
5 minced cloves of garlic
2 tablespoons ground cumin
1/2 cup red chili powder
2 large (28 ounce) cans diced tomatoes with juice
1 small can diced green chiles
2 cans pinto beans
2 cans red kidney beans
2 cans black beans
6 cups beef stock or water

Cook the bison meat in a large pot until done; drain off any excess drippings. Add the onion, garlic, cumin, and red chili powder and cook until the onion softens. Add the tomatoes, green chiles, beans, and beef stock or water. Bring to a boil. Lower heat to simmer and cook for another 30 minutes.

Wyoming's Folklore and Legends

Legends and folklore are stories that are not totally true but are often based on bits of truth. These stories help people understand things that are not easily explained. They also teach lessons to younger generations. All peoples have passed down stories as part of their culture.

The Crystal Mountain

A city fellow came to Wyoming to go hunting. After stopping for the night in a small town, he heard people talking about a crystal mountain so clear that no one could actually see it. "I've seen birds fly into it and drop dead," said one local. The hunter did not say anything, not wanting to offend the locals. "What a bunch of nonsense," he thought to himself. "There is no such thing as a clear crystal mountain." The next day, the hunter hiked down into the woods. Soon, he came to a clearing, where he saw a deer in the distance. He raised his rifle and fired at the deer, but missed it. He moved closer and fired yet again.

A moment later, the bullet whizzed back in his direction, barely missing him. "What?" he wondered. He moved ahead until he ran into an invisible wall, nearly breaking his nose. "So the crystal mountain is real," he said. He had not been firing at the deer but at its reflection in the clear crystal surface. "Guess that shows me not to question the people who have lived in Wyoming for a long time," he said, as he rubbed his nose.

Lost Gold

Three prospectors came to the Wind River Mountains because they heard that gold could be found everywhere in the area. Yet for days they searched and found no gold. Finally, about to give up, they camped by a stream and found some huge nuggets of gold. There was so much gold that they decided to bury it, so they might go home for more wagons and mules. On the journey home, two of the men died, leaving all of the gold for the survivor. He returned the next year with wagons and mules to dig up the treasure. He dug hole after hole, but he could not find the gold. He spent the rest of his life chasing the lost gold—without success. "Guess this is what happens when gold takes over your head," he later told his grandchildren. "Take it as a lesson. There are more important things than wasting your life searching for lost gold."

Wyoming's Sports Teams

Of all the 50 states, Wyoming is the only one with only one four-year college, the University of Wyoming. Also, it has no major-league professional teams. Local sports fans cheer for the university's teams.

Like other state universities, the University of Wyoming—the Cowboys—fields teams in football; men's and women's basketball, swimming, and track and field; wrestling; women's volleyball; baseball; and other sports.

The Cowboys' home games are played at the Double A basketball arena in Laramie. When filled, the arena is temporarily the fifth-largest city in the state.

College Basketball

In 1943 the Cowboys were the first team from the Rocky Mountains to win the National Collegiate Athletic Association (NCAA) basketball championship. This team was led by Kenny Sailors, the only basketball player in Wyoming history to earn All-American honors three times. Sailors, a native of Hillsdale, is credited with inventing the jump shot. In the late 1940s and early 1950s, he played five professional seasons in the National Basketball Association.

College Football

The Cowboys' football team plays home games in War Memorial Stadium. When filled, it is temporarily the third-largest city in the state. Cowboys football has a strong history. Led by quarterback and kicker Eddie Talboom, the Cowboys had a record of 9-1 in 1949 and a perfect 10-0 in 1950. Talboom became Wyoming's first All-American in football. He set thirteen Cowboy scoring records, including a single-game mark of 29 points in a 103-0 victory over Colorado State College in 1949. When he graduated, Talboom was the greatest scorer in NCAA history and still ranks among the highest-scoring football players ever.

The Wyoming Cowboys were undefeated at home during Jim Kiick's three seasons as starting tailback from 1965 to 1967.

Other famous Cowboys include running back Jim Kiick. After a star career as a Cowboy, Kiick joined the Miami Dolphins of the National Football League (NFL), where he played in the same backfield as fullback Larry Csonka and quarterback Bob Griese. The Dolphins won two Super Bowls and had a 17-0 record in 1972, the only perfect season in NFL history. Jay Novacek was a two-sport All-American in football and track and field. As a professional football player, Novacek won three Super Bowl championships as a member of the Dallas Cowboys.

Women's Volleyball

The Cowgirls women's volleyball team attracts players from Wyoming and surrounding states. Mary Shea, a

In recent years, snowboarding has challenged skiing as the most popular winter sport.

four-year volleyball starter, is considered one of the best athletes in the state's history. She set a number of Cowgirl records, including 486 "kills," or winning shots, in 1983, when the team won 27 matches.

Other sports

Skiing and snowboarding are popular recreational and competitive sports. The ski and snowboard runs at the Jackson Hole Mountain Resort in northwest Wyoming are considered among the best in the world. One unique ski event there is the Cowboy Ski Challenge each February. Skiers wear cowboy hats and leather chaps, or leg coverings, and race one another. They are pulled behind a horse and often reach speeds of 40 miles per hour.

Wyoming's Businesses and Products

People living in Wyoming work in a number of different jobs and industries. The state has three main industries: mining, agriculture, and tourism.

Mining and Quarrying

Mining is Wyoming's largest industry, bringing in more than $3.5 billion a year. Mining includes the removal of minerals, coal, oil, and gas from the ground. Quarrying is a special type of mining. It is the cutting of rock such as granite, which is used for covering buildings and paths.

Wyoming leads the nation in the production of bentonite. Bentonite is a claylike substance created by vol-

Wyoming produces more than 2 million tons of coal each year and ranks first in the nation in coal production.

Wyoming's Coal Mines

The two largest coal mines in the United States are located in Wyoming. Black Thunder opened in 1977 in the Southern Powder River Basin. Black Thunder was the largest coal mine until the nearby North Antelope Rochelle mine opened. The North Antelope mine began operation in late 1983, and the Rochelle mine began production in late 1985. The two mines merged in January 1999, making North Antelope Rochelle the largest coal-mining operation in the United States. More than 740 million tons of coal have been removed in the mine's history.

canoes. It is used by the oil-drilling industry and also is found in cosmetics, toothpaste, cement, water softeners, and fire extinguishers. The state also leads the world in the production of trona. Trona is a gray or white mineral used to make glass, paper, soaps, and other products. Wyoming is fourth in the nation in the production of crude oil and sixth in the production of natural gas.

The first coal mine in Wyoming opened in Carbon in 1867. The coal under Wyoming's central basins is estimated to last for 500 years. The coal is taken by rail to power generation plants, where it is burned to produce electricity used in western and southern states.

Agriculture

Agriculture brings $1.5 billion to Wyoming each year. The cattle industry makes up the largest part of the state's agricultural income, earning more than $400 million each year. About 35 million acres of the state are devoted to farming and ranching. More than 9,000 huge farms and ranches blanket the state. With an average about 3,700 acres each, Wyoming's farms and ranches are the largest in the country.

Other farm products are also important to Wyoming. The state is second in the nation in wool production, third in the number of sheep and lambs, seventh in the production of sugar beets, and ninth in barley. Other products include beans, hay, timber, corn, and wheat.

About fifteen percent of Wyoming's people, or 8,700 families, work in agriculture. Farming accounts for about ten percent of the state's total income.

Tourism

Yellowstone National Park, Jackson Hole ski resort, Grand Teton National Park, and Cheyenne Frontier Days are among the destinations that make tourism Wyoming's second most important industry. It brings in more than $1.57 billion a year, which is slightly more than what agriculture brings in. More than 28,000 people work in Wyoming's tourist industry.

About 2.5 million people visit Grand Teton National Park each year for its scenic natural beauty.

Attractions and Landmarks

Visitors come to Wyoming for its great outdoors. It is home to the world's largest elk herd and has more pronghorn antelope than anywhere else in North America. Pronghorn antelope are the fastest animals in North America. They can run at speeds of up to 60 miles per hour. They run nearly as fast as cheetahs, the fastest land animal in the world.

Medicine Wheel

Near the town of Lovell is one of the most mysterious remains of a late Native American culture—the Medicine Wheel. This circular rock formation dates back to about 1200. From above, it looks like an enormous wheel with 28 spokes. No one is certain who built it or why it was built.

THE WYOMING DINOSAUR CENTER AND DIG SITE

The Wyoming Dinosaur Center and Dig Site is huge. The Dinosaur Center houses about 12,000 square feet of exhibition area where fossils are displayed. More than 200 displays are shown, with twenty full-size mounted

Places to See in Wyoming

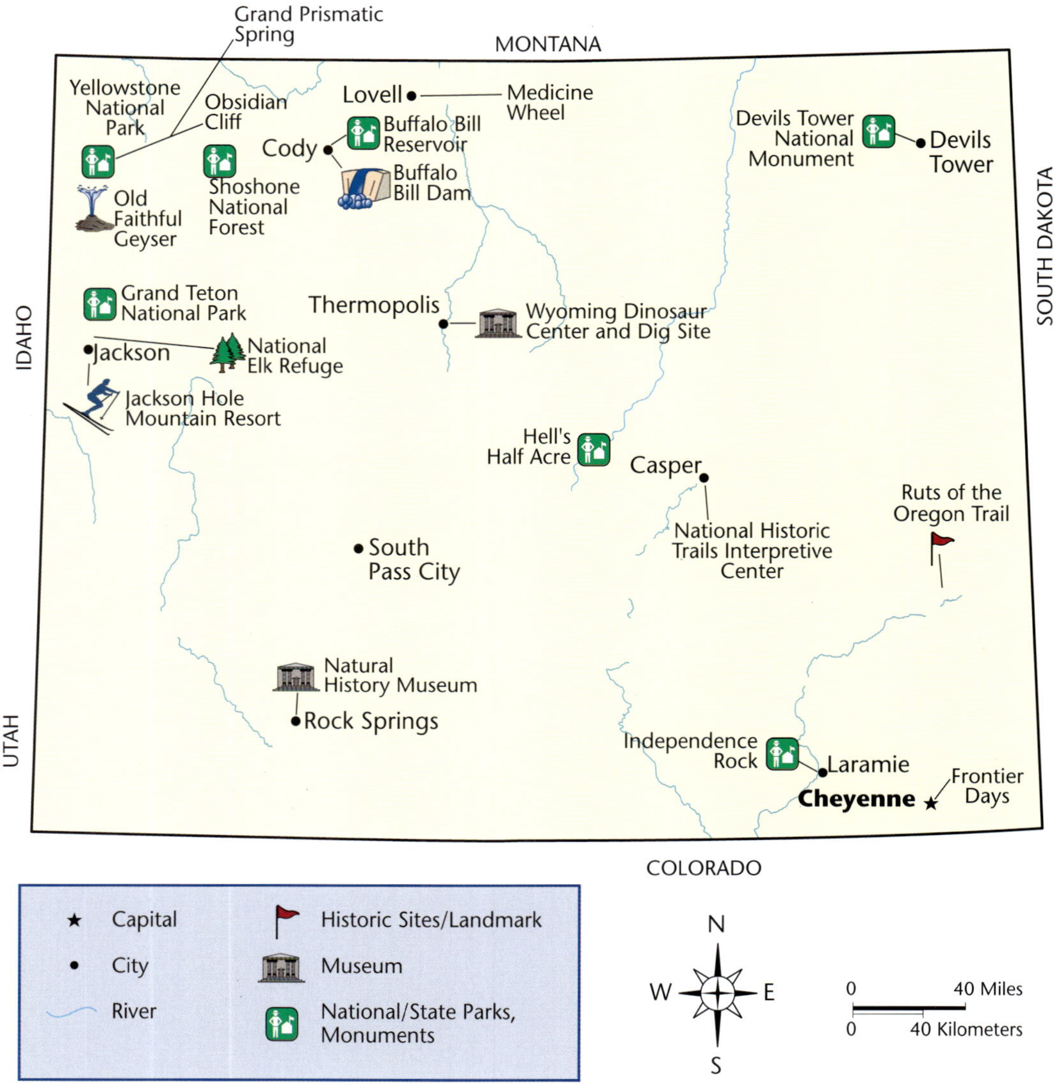

skeletons, including ten dinosaurs, in the central hall. At the dig quarries, visitors can discover, collect, and document Jurassic-era dinosaur fossils with the help of museum specialists.

The Wyoming Dinosaur Center and Dig Site is located on the Warm Springs Ranch in Thermopolis. The fossil-rich rocks were deposited during the Jurassic period—between 208 and 145 million years ago. This area contains one of the world's best places to find dinosaur fossils.

The Natural History Museum

The Natural History Museum, on the campus of Western Wyoming Community College in Rock Springs, is home to a large collection of dinosaur fossils, including several complete skeletons. People have come to Wyoming in search of fossil remains since the 1870s. Many fossils were found in Como, including the triceratops. Today paleontologists, scientists who study ancient life, continue to work on dig sites in Wyoming.

The National Historic Trails Interpretive Center

The National Historic Trails Interpretive Center opened in Casper in August 2002. Wyoming was chosen as the site for this center because so many westward trails went through the state. It hosts interactive exhibits on the Native Americans, the **Oregon Trail,** the **California Trail,** the Mormon Trail, the Overland Trail, and the Pony Express. Visitors can prepare for a wagon train trip by deciding what to pack and then relive pioneer experiences such as fording a river. A part of the center shows the trails as they look today—which is almost exactly as they looked more than 100 years ago.

Independence Rock

Located 55 miles southwest of Casper, Independence Rock is a large granite outcropping that rises above the plains. An unknown explorer carved the word *Independence* on the rock to honor the United States. Afterward, many more people followed his idea. About 50,000 names were carved or painted on the rock during the mid-1800s. It remains a record of the people who passed through Wyoming on their way west.

Devils Tower was featured in the Steven Spielberg movie Close Encounters of the Third Kind.

Devils Tower

In 1906 Devils Tower became the first national monument. It is in northeast Wyoming, at the western edge of the Black Hills that range into South Dakota. The site is sacred to many Native Americans. Devils Tower played an important role in the legends and folklore of Native Americans. It was considered a place where energy gathered. Today the National Park Service manages Devils Tower. More than 400,000 visitors come to the tower each year.

The National Elk Refuge

Established in 1912, the National Elk Refuge is located two miles north of Jackson in northwestern Wyoming. It covers 25,000 acres and contains nearly 10,000 elk during the winter feeding season. A herd of about 700 bison also winter in the refuge. Scientists at the refuge have identified more than 47 different types of mammals and 175 kinds of birds. Between November and May, it is the best place in Wyoming to observe wildlife.

Hell's Half Acre

Forty-five miles west of Casper is a strange collection of colorful, deeply eroded landforms. The area is called Hell's Half Acre because the rocks here were burned a long time ago when underground coal deposits caught fire. Surrounded by mountains and valleys, the area is a public park covering about 300 acres (despite its name). In 1996 the site was used for the science-fiction movie *Starship Troopers,* where a space city was temporarily built on the formation.

Jackson Hole and Grand Teton National Park

Jackson Hole is a 50-mile long valley surrounded by high mountains in northwestern Wyoming. Jackson, with about 8,500 people, is the only town in the valley. Jackson Hole is known for its mountains, valleys, and ski trails. In addition to being a popular place for outdoor activities, Jackson Hole has more than 30 art galleries. Jackson Hole attracts more than 3 million visitors a year.

Grand Teton National Park, established in 1929, is located within Jackson Hole, about 56 miles north of Jackson. The park is known for the jagged Teton Range that hovers over the valley. The highest peak, the Grand Teton, soars to 13,770 feet, almost 7,500 feet above the valley floor. A chain of lakes below the Tetons provide scenic hiking trails and clear waters for canoeing or boating.

Jackson Hole, in northwestern Wyoming, attracts more than 3 million visitors each year. Jackson is named after a trapper, David E. Jackson. A "hole" is what mountain men called a large valley ringed by mountains.

Obsidian Cliff

Located in Yellowstone National Park is Obsidian Cliff. It is a mountain of shiny black glass. The glass was formed as a volcano released one of the largest deposits of **obsidian** in North America. The rock first melted and then quickly cooled. Native Americans used obsidian in arrowheads and jewelry.

Grand Prismatic Spring

Another Yellowstone National Park wonder is the Grand Prismatic Spring. It is the largest hot spring in the park and the third-largest hot spring in the world. Heated water gently flows from the earth and spreads out in layers of color. The pond created by the spring appears as a vibrating rainbow, with its colors and patterns continuously changing.

The presence of microscopic, heat-loving organisms called thermophiles gives Grand Prismatic Spring its rainbow-like colors.

Map of Wyoming

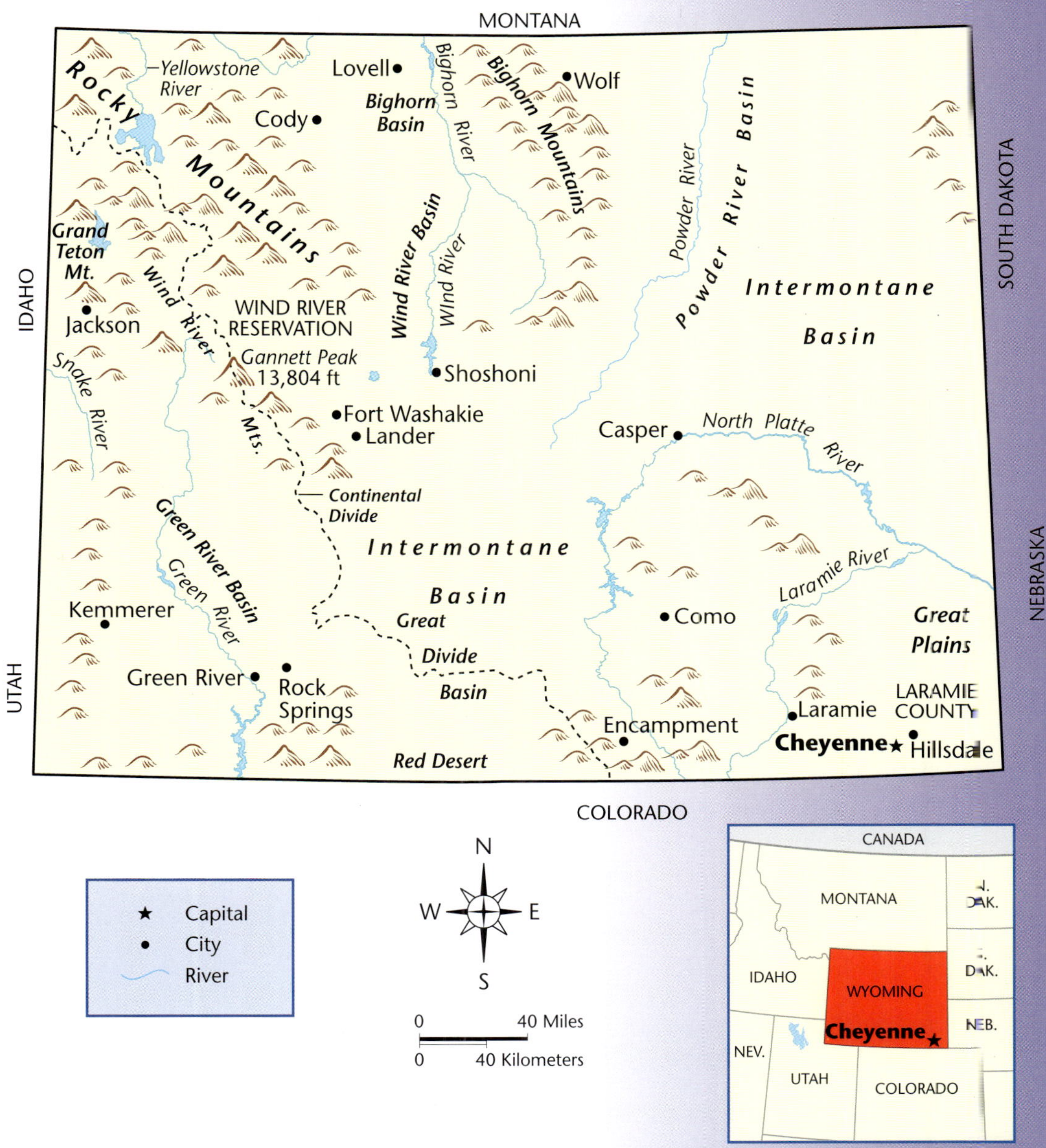

Glossary

abstract a type of art that uses lines, shapes, and symbols

appeals cases a court case that the defendant asks a higher court to review

artifacts objects made by humans hands, usually primitive art or tools

bailiff an officer whose job is maintaining order in the courtroom

bills proposals for new laws

buttes steep hills with flat tops

California Trail name given to a branch of the Oregon Trail, beginning in southern Idaho, that led to California

civil cases court actions between individuals having to do with private rights rather than criminal action

continental divide a mountainous region where the rivers on either side flow in opposite directions

criminal cases court actions dealing with violations of the law

dormitory college housing for students

elevation the distance above sea level

erosion the wearing away of land by wind, water, or weather conditions

geysers natural hot springs that shoot a spray of water and steam into the air

legislature a group of elected officials who make laws for a state or nation

magma molten rock under the earth's crust

majority more than half

Mormons members of the Church of Jesus Christ of Latter-day Saints, which was founded by Joseph Smith in 1830

mountain men explorers and adventurers who lived in the mountains during the 1800s, and survived by hunting animals for food and fur. Many mountain men also sold their fur to make a living.

nonpartisan not belonging to or supporting one political party

obsidian a black volcanic glass

Oregon Trail name given to a number of wagon roads leading west from Missouri to the Oregon Territory; branches of the trail lead to California, Utah, and other western destinations

override to overrule a veto by means of a two-thirds majority vote of both houses of the legislature

pelts animal furs

prospectors explorers who looked for gold and other valuable minerals

secret ballot a vote cast secretly so that no one knows who the voter choses

transcontinental spanning the continent

treaties formal agreements between two or more nations, often used to divide land, end a war, or establish trade

veto to prevent a bill from becoming a law by rejecting it

More Books to Read

Bell, Mary Reeves. *The Sagebrush Rebellion.* Bloomington, Minn.: Bethany House, 1999.

Ehrlich, Gretel. *A Blizzard Year: Timmy's Almanac of Seasons.* New York: Hyperion Press, 1999.

Naylor, Phyllis Reynolds. *Walker's Crossing.* New York: Atheneum Press, 1999.

Schaefer, Jack. *Shane.* Boston: Houghton Mifflin, 2001.

Wooldridge, Connie Nordhielm. *When Esther Morris Headed West: Women, Wyoming, and the Right to Vote.* New York: Holiday House, 2001.

Index

agriculture, 37-38
Atkinson, Mary, 11

bentonite, 36
bison, 6, 15
Bozeman, John M., 18
Buffalo Bill Dam, 11
Buffalo Chili (recipe), 30

Campbell, Robert, 9
Casper, 5, 41
Cheney, Dick, 21
Cheyenne, 4, 18, 25, 27
Cheyenne Frontier Days, 27, 38
chuck wagon, 29
climate, 7
coal, 36, 37
Colter, John, 16-17
continental divide, 6, 7
cottonwood, 14
courts, 26
Cowboy Ski Challenge, 35
culture, 27-28
cutthroat trout, 14

Devils Tower, 10, 42
Dodge, Grenville, 4
Downey, June Etta, 19
dude ranch, 9-10

Eaton Ranch, 9

folklore, 31-32
food, 29-30
Fort William, 9

geography, 6-7
ghost towns, 27-28
Goodnight, Charles, 29
government, 24-26
  executive branch, 25
  judicial branch, 26
  legislative branch, 24-25
Gowdy, Curt, 20
Grand Prismatic Spring, 44
Grand Teton, 43
Grand Teton National Park, 38, 43
Great Plains, 6, 7

Hell's Half Acre, 43
history, 16-18
horned lizard, 15

Independence Rock, 41
Indian paintbrush, 13
Intermontane Basin, 6-7

Jackson, 11
Jackson Hole, 43
Jackson Hole Mountain Resort, 35, 38

Laramie, 5, 18, 33
Lewis and Clark Expedition, 16
library system, 11

Medicine Wheel, 39
mining, 36-37
Mormon Trail, 18, 41
Morris, Esther Hobart, 10

National Elk Refuge, 42
National Historic Trails Interpretive Center, 41
Native Americans, 4, 9, 10, 16-17, 19, 41, 42, 44
Natural History Museum, 41

Obsidian Cliff, 44
Oregon Trail, 17, 41

Penny, James Cash, 10
Pollock, Jackson, 20
pronghorn antelope, 39

railroads, 4, 18
Red Desert, 8
Rocky Mountains, 6
Ross, Nellie Tayloe, 19
Russin, Robert, 5

Sailors, Kenny, 33
Shea, Mary, 34
Shoshone National Forest, 10
Simpson, Alan, 20-21
South Pass City, 28
sports, 11, 33-35
state symbols
  bird, 14
  dinosaur, 15
  fish, 14
  flag, 12
  flower, 13
  mammal, 15
  motto, 12
  nicknames, 12-13
  reptile, 15
  seal, 12
  song, 13
  tree, 14
statehood, 18
Sublette, William, 9

Talboom, Eddie, 34
tourism, 38
triceratops, 15, 41

University of Wyoming, 5, 33
University of Wyoming Cowboys, 33-34
University of Wyoming Cowgirls, 34-35

Washakie, 19
western meadowlark, 14
Wind River reservation, 16
Wolf, 9
wolf reintroduction, 23
women's rights, 4, 10-11, 18
Wyoming Dinosaur Center and Dig Site, 39-41
"Wyoming" (song), 13
Wyoming Territory, 4

Yellowstone National Park, 9, 17, 22-23, 38, 44

About the Authors

Larry Bograd is the author of many books for children and young adults. He was born in Denver, Colorado, and now lives there with his wife and three daughters. He has traveled throughout Wyoming.

D.J. Ross is a writer and educator with more than 25 years of experience in education. Ross has lived throughout the United States and now lives in the Midwest with his three basset hounds.